Olympiad ACE

A Comprehensive Practice Book

for School Olympiads & Talent Search Exams

COMPUTER

Class 1

by
Debapriya Chakraborty

Bloom Cap Edu Ventures Pvt. Ltd.

卐 **Administrative & Production Office**

'Ramchhaya' 4577/15, Agarwal Road, Darya Ganj, New Delhi -110002
Tele: 011- 47630600, 43518550

卐 **PRICE :** ₹125.00

卐 **PO No :** TXT-XX-XXXXXXX-X-XX

Published by Arihant Publications (I) Ltd.

For further information about the books log on to
www.bloomcap.org

Follow us on 

Preface

"Future belongs to those Who prepares for it today"

School Olympiads are National & International level competitions conducted by different Government, Non-Government & Educational Organisations with the purpose of making the children ready to face competitive exams.

The challenging Questions asked in Olympiads motivate them to learn more & more and bring out the best result with improved academic performance. The Awards & Scholarship offered by Olympiads motivate children to aspire & strive for doing better and emerge out to be the best.

Science Olympiads

Being a Scientist or Engineer or Doctor has always been a dream of each school going child. A good command over Science is a must for any of these. Questions of Science Olympiads are structured to help students to develop scientific temperament & motivate them to understand the concepts of science. They also focuses on improving existing knowledge of a student by adding more information.

'Bloom Science Olympiad Study Book Class 1' is a perfect resource to Study & Practice for Olympiad Exams and other National & State Level Talent Search Exams & Other Competitions.

Some Special Features of Bloom Science Olympiad Study Books are;

- Chapterwise Exercises having different types of Objective Questions; Analytical, Applications, Remembering etc, at par with the Olympiad Level.
- Detailed Explanation for each question.
- Olympiad Pattern Practice Sets at the end.

This book is prepared by Expert Panel with the utmost care, still if you have any suggestions regarding its improvement then feel free to contact us at support@bloomcap.org. We will try to inculcate your suggestions in the further editions.

Contents

01

Introduction to Computer

1. Which of the following things a computer cannot do?

    (a) Work fast   (b) Do many tasks at a time

    (c) Learn new things   (d) Do sums

2. What can a computer do?

    (a) Store information   (b) Learn new things

    (c) Think of new games   (d) Do task of its own

3. What is common between Man and Computer?

    (a) Both can get tired.

    (b) Both can draw and calculate.

    (c) Both can take decisions.

    (d) Both can show emotions.

4. Tick the activity that a computer can help us in doing.

(a) 
    (b) 

5. The machine which can do work of a computer is

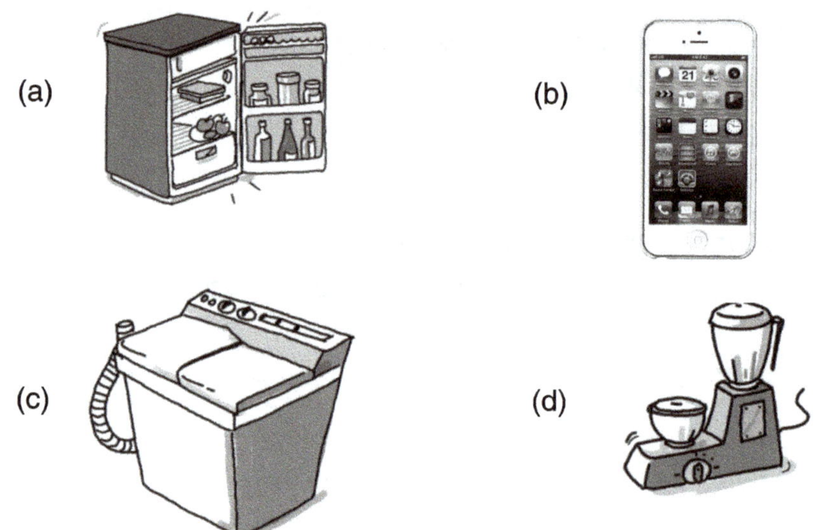

Directions (Q. No. 6-7) See the image given below and answer the following.

6. How many laptops and desktops are there?
   (a) Laptop=3, Desktop=2   (b) Laptop=2, Desktop=3
   (c) Laptop=2, Desktop=1   (d) Laptop=1, Desktop=2

7. How many tablets and mobiles are there?
   (a) Tablet=1, Mobile=3   (b) Tablet=2, Mobile=4
   (c) Tablet=4, Mobile=3   (d) Tablet=3, Mobile=1

8. Computers are used in schools for keeping
   (a) tickets   (b) fee records
   (c) music   (d) games

9. Identify the incorrect statement from the following.
   (a) An aeroplane is a machine.
   (b) Machines do not save our time.
   (c) A washing machine runs on electricity.
   (d) A computer makes no mistakes.

10. Visual Display Unit (VDU) is also called
    (a) Scanner   (b) CPU
    (c) Monitor   (d) Printer

11. Which one of the following devices produce sound when connected with the computer?

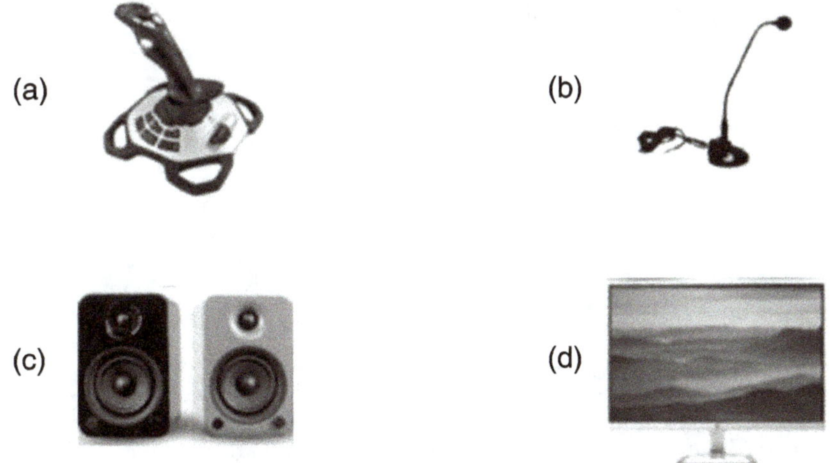

(a)   (b)

(c)   (d)

12. Which one of the following is the set of three basic parts of a computer?

(a) Printer, Input and Output

(b) Scanner, Input and Output

(c) Input, Processing and Output

(d) None of the above

13. With this capability, computers can perform the same operations tirelessly and repeatedly.

(a) Speed   (b) Accuracy

(c) Repetitiveness   (d) Self-Checking

14. With which capability, computers can process data very fast?

(a) Store and Recall   (b) Logical Operations

(c) Accuracy   (d) Speed

15. A .... is a metal or plastic box that contains the main components of a computer.

(a) Computer box   (b) Computer holder

(c) Computer case   (d) None of these

16. Choose the incorrect statement.

(a) We can play games on a computer.

(b) A computer can be used to solve sums.

(c) We use pen and pencil to draw in computer.

(d) We can watch movies on a computer.

Darken your choice with HB Pencil

1.	ⓐ ⓑ ⓒ ⓓ	5.	ⓐ ⓑ ⓒ ⓓ	9.	ⓐ ⓑ ⓒ ⓓ	13.	ⓐ ⓑ ⓒ ⓓ
2.	ⓐ ⓑ ⓒ ⓓ	6.	ⓐ ⓑ ⓒ ⓓ	10.	ⓐ ⓑ ⓒ ⓓ	14.	ⓐ ⓑ ⓒ ⓓ
3.	ⓐ ⓑ ⓒ ⓓ	7.	ⓐ ⓑ ⓒ ⓓ	11.	ⓐ ⓑ ⓒ ⓓ	15.	ⓐ ⓑ ⓒ ⓓ
4.	ⓐ ⓑ ⓒ ⓓ	8.	ⓐ ⓑ ⓒ ⓓ	12.	ⓐ ⓑ ⓒ ⓓ	16.	ⓐ ⓑ ⓒ ⓓ

02

Parts of a Computer

1. The .... controls the computer.
   - (a) mouse
   - (b) CPU
   - (c) monitor
   - (d) keyboard

2. Choose the name of the device shown in the following picture.

   - (a) Monitor
   - (b) Mouse
   - (c) Keyboard
   - (d) None of these

3. Which device is used to print words and pictures from computer?
   - (a) Printer
   - (b) Speaker
   - (c) Mouse
   - (d) Monitor

4. We can move the pointer (▷) on the screen using the
   - (a) keyboard
   - (b) monitor
   - (c) mouse
   - (d) hand

5. We can enter letters and numbers into the computer using the
   - (a) keyboard
   - (b) monitor
   - (c) mouse
   - (d) CPU

6. Which part of the computer is/are correctly matched to your body part?

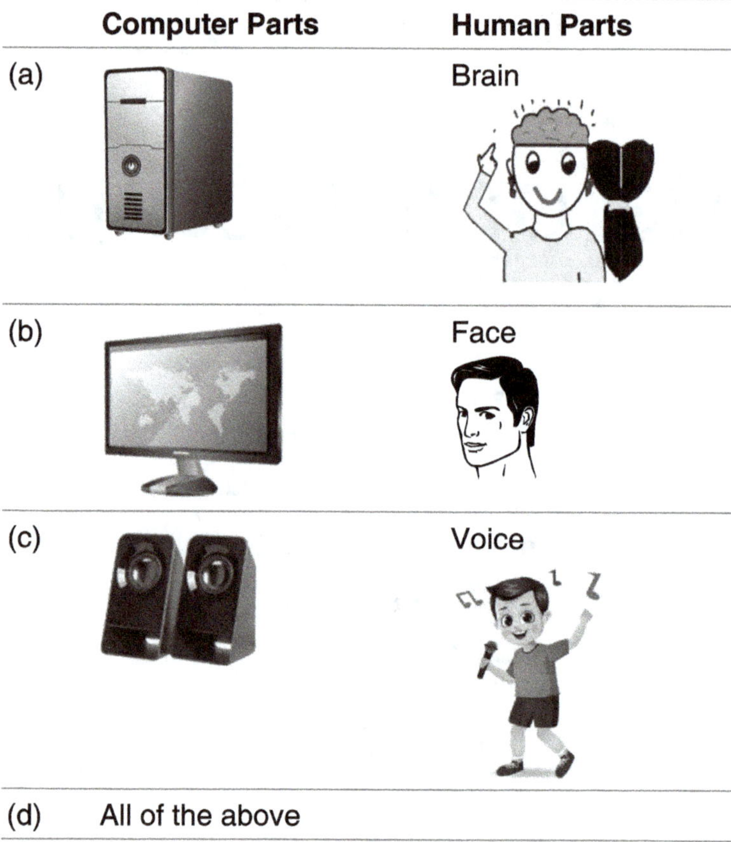

	Computer Parts	Human Parts
(a)		Brain
(b)		Face
(c)		Voice

(d)   All of the above

7. .... has/have two or three buttons.

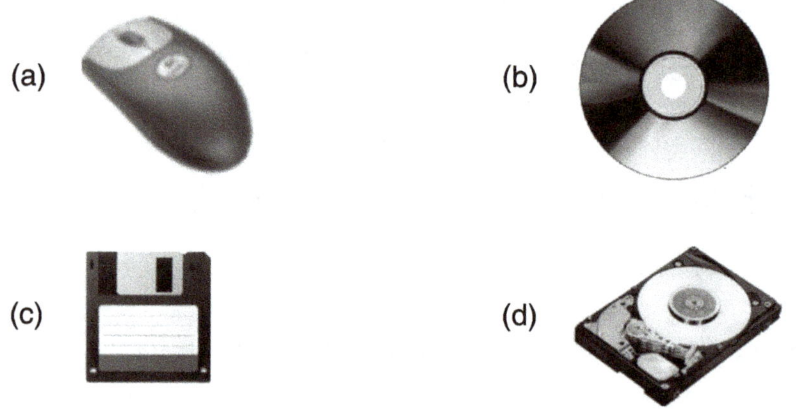

(a)   (b)

(c)   (d)

8. Identify the correct part of the computer from the jumbled word given below.

DRAYOBEK

(a) 

(b) 

(c) 

(d) 

9. What is the component that helps us hear the audio output from a computer?
   (a) Monitor   (b) USB
   (c) Speakers   (d) Hard disk

10. It is a listening device with two small speakers held to the ear by a band over the head.

   (a) Microphone   (b) Headphone
   (c) Speaker   (d) Web camera

11. Select the pair of three input devices your computer uses.
   (a) Mouse, Keyboard, Monitor   (b) Mouse, Keyboard, Scanner
   (c) Mouse, Printer, CPU   (d) Mouse, Scanner, Printer

12. Physical components that make up your computer are known as
   (a) software   (b) hardware
   (c) operating systems   (d) web browsers

13. Which of the following is not an input device?

(a) Keyboard

(b) Joystick

(c) Monitor

(d) Microphone

14. Which storage device is shown in picture?

(a) Memory Card

(b) Flash Drive

(c) Hard Disk

(d) Compact Disk

15. Identify this storage device.

(a) Pen Drive

(b) Memory Card

(c) CD

(d) Hard drive

16. The monitor is an output device or display device. Which one of the following is a type of monitor?

(a) TFT Monitor

(b) LCD Monitor

(c) LED Monitor

(d) All of these

17. This is the ICON for

(a) fortnight

(b) turning the computer on or off

(c) the clock

(d) the settings

18. Choose the correct names of the parts of a computer marked as A, B, C, D.

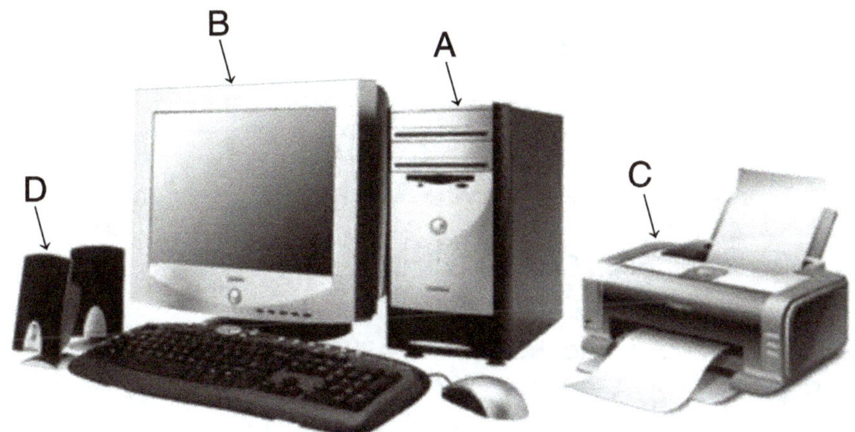

(a) A-CPU, B-Monitor, C-Printer, D-Speakers

(b) A-Printer, B-Speakers, C-CPU, D-Monitor

(c) A-Monitor, B-Speakers, C-CPU, D-Printer

(d) A-Printer, B-CPU, C-Speakers, D-Monitor

19. Identify the following keys marked on the Keyboard.

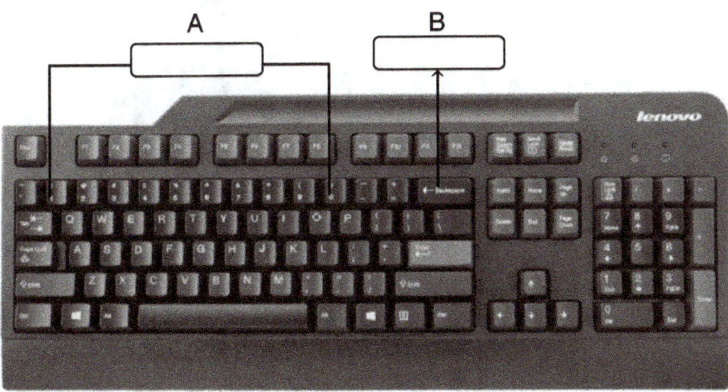

(a) A-Alphabet and B-Function

(b) A-Alphabet and B-Numbers

(c) A-Numbers and B-Backspace

(d) A-Alphabet and B-Backspace

20. Label the parts of a Mouse given in the following figure.

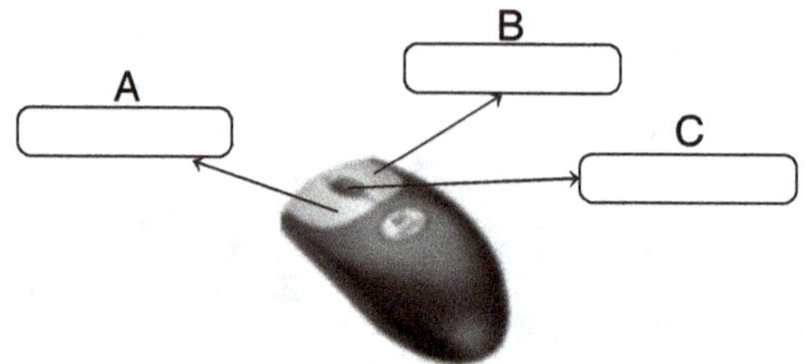

(a) A-Left Click, B-Right Click, C-Scroll Wheel
(b) A-Right Click, B-Left Click, C-Scroll Wheel
(c) A- Scroll Wheel, B-Right Click, C- Left Click
(d) A-Right Click, B- Scroll Wheel, C-Left Click

21. Identify the device by the following description.

I. It is the brain of a computer.

II. It helps a computer to think and work according to the given orders.

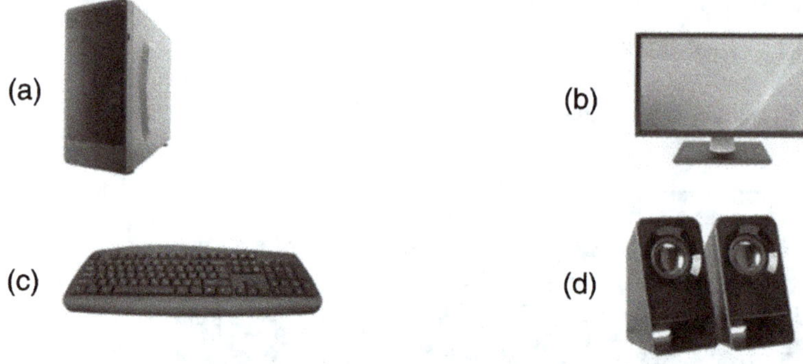

(a)

(b)

(c)

(d)

Darken your choice with HB Pencil

1.	ⓐ ⓑ ⓒ ⓓ	5.	ⓐ ⓑ ⓒ ⓓ	9.	ⓐ ⓑ ⓒ ⓓ	13.	ⓐ ⓑ ⓒ ⓓ	17.	ⓐ ⓑ ⓒ ⓓ	21.	ⓐ ⓑ ⓒ ⓓ
2.	ⓐ ⓑ ⓒ ⓓ	6.	ⓐ ⓑ ⓒ ⓓ	10.	ⓐ ⓑ ⓒ ⓓ	14.	ⓐ ⓑ ⓒ ⓓ	18.	ⓐ ⓑ ⓒ ⓓ		
3.	ⓐ ⓑ ⓒ ⓓ	7.	ⓐ ⓑ ⓒ ⓓ	11.	ⓐ ⓑ ⓒ ⓓ	15.	ⓐ ⓑ ⓒ ⓓ	19.	ⓐ ⓑ ⓒ ⓓ		
4.	ⓐ ⓑ ⓒ ⓓ	8.	ⓐ ⓑ ⓒ ⓓ	12.	ⓐ ⓑ ⓒ ⓓ	16.	ⓐ ⓑ ⓒ ⓓ	20.	ⓐ ⓑ ⓒ ⓓ		

03

Uses of Computer

1. I am used for sending E-Mails. Who am I?

(a) 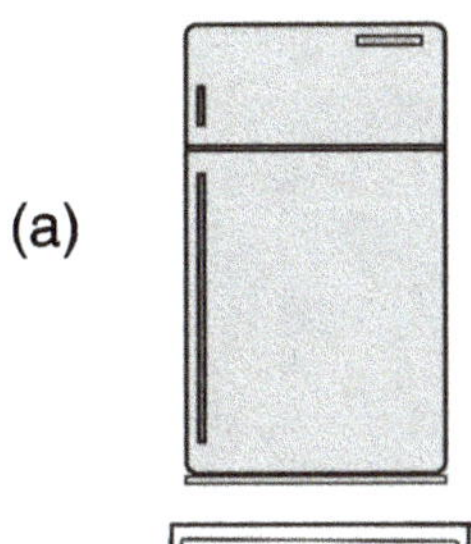

(b) 

(c) 

(d) 

2. Computer is used in shopping malls for

(a) reservation

(b) billing

(c) observation

(d) manipulation

3. Computers are not used in

(a) 

(b) 

(c)

(d)

4. Computer helps in entertainment by letting us
   (a) listen to music   (b) play games
   (c) watch cartoon   (d) All of these

5. Our hands should be clean and .... before we touch computer.
   (a) wet   (b) dry
   (c) sticky   (d) dirty

6. Which of the following is used to withdraw money?

(a) 

(b) 

(c) 

(d)   All of these

7. Select the work which you cannot do on a computer.
   (a) Play games   (b) Draw cartoon
   (c) Swim   (d) Play music

8. Computers are used in a .... to store information about the books.
   (a) railway station   (b) library
   (c) banks   (d) resorts

9. Which of the following is used to play computer games?

(a) Printer   (b) Joystick

(c) Scanner   (d) Monitor

10. Find the name of a place where computers are used to book tickets from the following scrambled words.

(a) PSNIOPHG LALM

(b) TSOP OFCFIE

(c) RBYIRAL

(d) AYAIRLW TTAISNO

11. Which of the following statements is incorrect?

(a) In hospitals, a computer does not help the doctor in operations.

(b) At home, you can use the computer to play games and do your homework.

(c) Computer helps in preparing medical records.

(d) The computer helps you with typing and printing documents.

12. Based on the picture, the computer can

(a) only send letters and play music

(b) only play some music

(c) do a lot of things at the same time

(d) do nothing

13. The story of computer started with the Abacus. What is the Abacus used for?

(a) Identifying different colors

(b) Exercising the hand muscles

(c) Adding and subtracting numbers

(d) Improving eye sight

Darken your choice with HB Pencil

1.	ⓐ ⓑ ⓒ ⓓ	5.	ⓐ ⓑ ⓒ ⓓ	9.	ⓐ ⓑ ⓒ ⓓ	13.	ⓐ ⓑ ⓒ ⓓ
2.	ⓐ ⓑ ⓒ ⓓ	6.	ⓐ ⓑ ⓒ ⓓ	10.	ⓐ ⓑ ⓒ ⓓ		
3.	ⓐ ⓑ ⓒ ⓓ	7.	ⓐ ⓑ ⓒ ⓓ	11.	ⓐ ⓑ ⓒ ⓓ		
4.	ⓐ ⓑ ⓒ ⓓ	8.	ⓐ ⓑ ⓒ ⓓ	12.	ⓐ ⓑ ⓒ ⓓ		

04

Introduction to Keyboard

1. There are .... shift keys on a typical keyboard.
    (a) 1   (b) 2
    (c) 3   (d) 4

2. Identify the following key and select how many such keys are there on a keyboard.

    (a) 1   (b) 2
    (c) 3   (d) 4

3. .... key is used to type capital letters when caps lock is off.
    (a) Enter   (b) Control
    (c) Shift   (d) Alter

4. .... is the shortcut key to make the selected text italic.
    (a) Ctrl + B   (b) Ctrl + I
    (c) Ctrl + U   (d) Ctrl + A

5. Which key can be pressed to erase your typing?

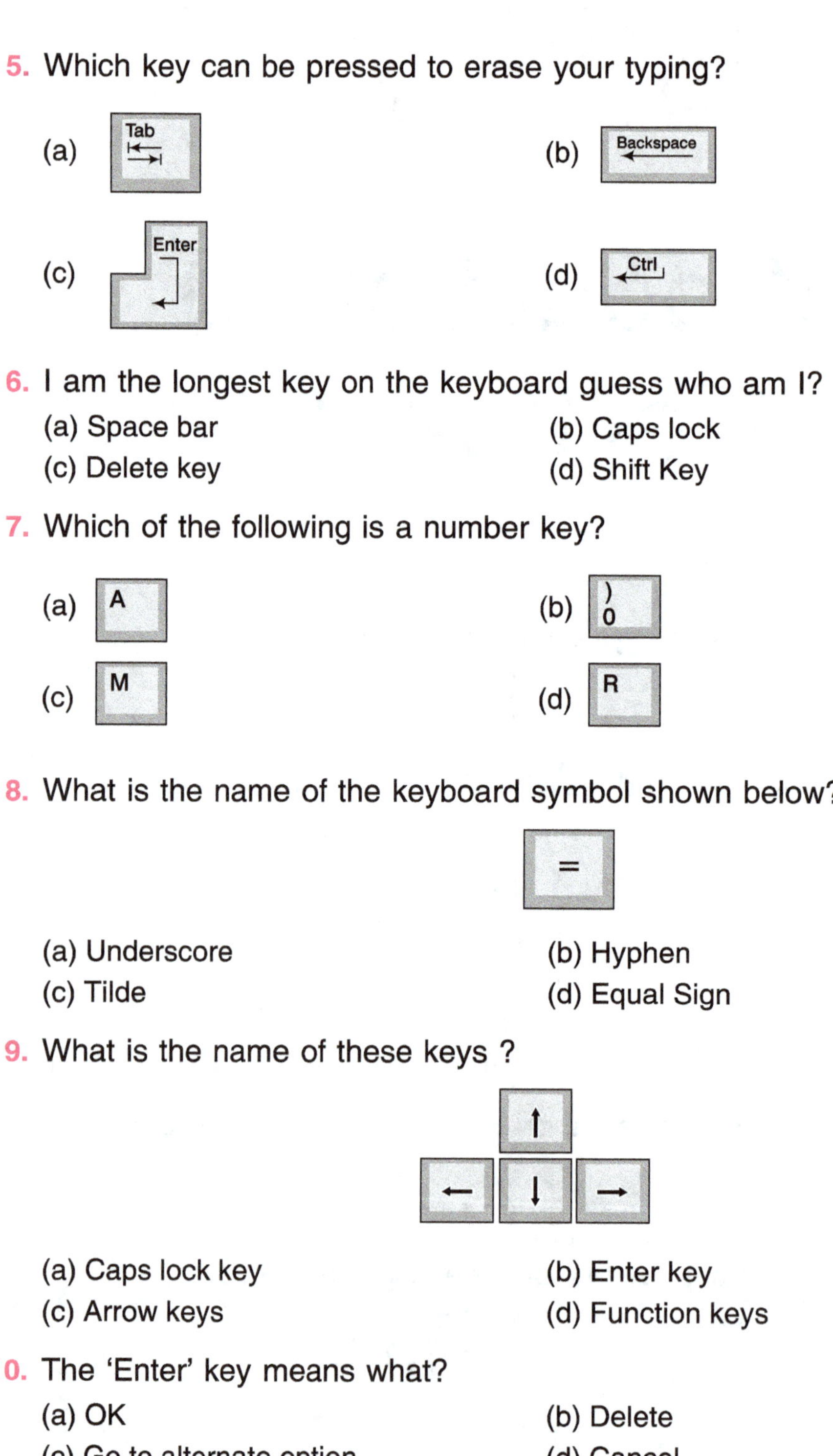

(a) (b)

(c) (d)

6. I am the longest key on the keyboard guess who am I?
   (a) Space bar   (b) Caps lock
   (c) Delete key   (d) Shift Key

7. Which of the following is a number key?

   (a)   (b)

   (c)   (d)

8. What is the name of the keyboard symbol shown below?

   (a) Underscore   (b) Hyphen
   (c) Tilde   (d) Equal Sign

9. What is the name of these keys ?

   (a) Caps lock key   (b) Enter key
   (c) Arrow keys   (d) Function keys

10. The 'Enter' key means what?
    (a) OK   (b) Delete
    (c) Go to alternate option   (d) Cancel

11. Instructions that tell the hardware what to do?

(a) Internet   (b) RAM

(c) Software   (d) Cursor

12. What is the function of 'Shift' key?

(a) Makes all letters capital.

(b) Makes one letter capital at a time.

(c) Jumps to the next important part of the screen.

(d) Erases all of the previous work.

13. The function of 'Tab' key is to

(a) advance the cursor to the next tap stop.

(b) go ahead or do the next thing.

(c) make all of the letters capital.

(d) make the screen look like it would if it were a tablet.

14. `Ctrl` + `D` What is this shortcut?

(a) Duplicate   (b) Select All

(c) Bold   (d) Copy

15. Which of these keys are on the top row?

(a) ZXCVB   (b) ASDFGH

(c) QWERTY   (d) ABCDEFG

16. Which of the following key is incorrectly matched with its function?

	Keys	Functions
(a)	Arrow	To move page down.
(b)	Enter	To go to next line of typing.
(c)	Spacebar	To put space between words while typing.
(d)	Page Up	To move up a page.

Darken your choice with HB Pencil

1.	(a) (b) (c) (d)	5.	(a) (b) (c) (d)	9.	(a) (b) (c) (d)	13.	(a) (b) (c) (d)
2.	(a) (b) (c) (d)	6.	(a) (b) (c) (d)	10.	(a) (b) (c) (d)	14.	(a) (b) (c) (d)
3.	(a) (b) (c) (d)	7.	(a) (b) (c) (d)	11.	(a) (b) (c) (d)	15.	(a) (b) (c) (d)
4.	(a) (b) (c) (d)	8.	(a) (b) (c) (d)	12.	(a) (b) (c) (d)	16.	(a) (b) (c) (d)

Introduction to Computer Mouse

1. A computer mouse is used for
   (a) drawing
   (b) creating lines
   (c) selecting options
   (d) All of these

2. Which of the following computer devices is similar to a mouse?
   (a) Joystick
   (b) Keyboard
   (c) Trackball
   (d) Barcode reader

3. A computer mouse is an essential part of
   (a) software
   (b) hardware
   (c) CPU
   (d) motherboard

4. Computer mouse is also known as .... device.
   (a) helping
   (b) typing
   (c) pointing
   (d) painting

5. When you move the mouse, the .... also moves in the same direction on the monitor screen.
   (a) arrow/cursor
   (b) key
   (c) image
   (d) None of these

6. The arrow in the picture is pointing at the

(a) body   (b) cursor
(c) scroll wheel   (d) left button

7. What is shown in the given image?

(a) Tool   (b) Cursor
(c) Mouse   (d) Window

8. Name button number 2 in the given picture.

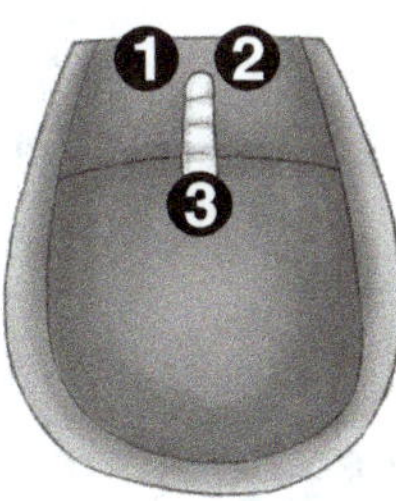

(a) Right button   (b) Left button
(c) Top click   (d) Bottom click

9. If you want to move an icon or object on the screen to other place or location on the screen then you,
   (a) Left Click   (b) Right Click
   (c) Double Click   (d) Drag and Drop

10. A computer mouse is used to

(a) write on a computer

(b) supply power to the computer

(c) select and open program on a computer

(d) Cook on a computer

11. There is a .... wheel in the center of a mouse.

(a) fixed   (b) scroll

(c) two   (d) scrool

12. A mouse is kept on a special sheet called

(a) keypad   (b) notepad

(c) mouse pad   (d) numeric pad

13. Which of the following is a correct way to hold a mouse?

(a)

(b)

(c)   (d) None of these

14. Which shapes moves on the computer screen when you move a mouse?

(a)

(b)

(c)

(d)

15. Which of the following you cannot do with a mouse?

(a) Point at the items

(b) Click on items

(c) Moving one item from one place to other

(d) Typing texts

16. What is incorrect about a mouse?

(a) A mouse is a pointing device. A mouse enables us to point at and click on the items.

(b) Clicking right button twice is called a click.

(c) We should keep the mouse on a mouse pad.

(d) Mouse without a wire is called a wireless mouse.

17. Which of the following sentence is incorrect about a computer mouse?

(a) We need to click the left button on the mouse to drag an object on computer monitor.

(b) A mouse communicates with the computer through cursor.

(c) A mouse needs a pad to place it.

(d) There are three buttons on a computer mouse.

Darken your choice with HB Pencil

1.	ⓐ ⓑ ⓒ ⓓ	5.	ⓐ ⓑ ⓒ ⓓ	9.	ⓐ ⓑ ⓒ ⓓ	13.	ⓐ ⓑ ⓒ ⓓ	17.	ⓐ ⓑ ⓒ ⓓ
2.	ⓐ ⓑ ⓒ ⓓ	6.	ⓐ ⓑ ⓒ ⓓ	10.	ⓐ ⓑ ⓒ ⓓ	14.	ⓐ ⓑ ⓒ ⓓ		
3.	ⓐ ⓑ ⓒ ⓓ	7.	ⓐ ⓑ ⓒ ⓓ	11.	ⓐ ⓑ ⓒ ⓓ	15.	ⓐ ⓑ ⓒ ⓓ		
4.	ⓐ ⓑ ⓒ ⓓ	8.	ⓐ ⓑ ⓒ ⓓ	12.	ⓐ ⓑ ⓒ ⓓ	16.	ⓐ ⓑ ⓒ ⓓ		

Starting and Shutting Down the Computer

1. What is the first step to start a computer?
   (a) Switch on the monitor.
   (b) Press the power button on UPS.
   (c) Press the power button on CPU.
   (d) Switch on the main power button.

2. You should always follow the correct steps to .... down your computer safely.
   (a) turn
   (b) shut
   (c) put
   (d) start

3. Make sure you have .... all programs before shutting the computer down.
   (a) finish
   (b) turn
   (c) closed
   (d) switch

4. If you do not shut down your computer correctly, you could .... your work!
   (a) loose
   (b) lose
   (c) save
   (d) cut

5. You should sit upright and use good.............while working on a computer.
   (a) colors
   (b) English
   (c) posture
   (d) software

6. To login, which of the following is typed into the computer alongwith username?

    (a) Email address   (b) Telephone Number

    (c) Hello   (d) Password

7. What is the last step to shut down a computer?

    (a) Switch off the monitor by pressing the power button on it.

    (b) Switch off the power switch.

    (c) Switch off UPS by pressing the power button on it.

    (d) Click on the start button and click on the shutdown option.

8. Which button on CPU helps you in turning on a computer?

    (a) Refresh   (b) Power

    (c) USB port   (d) None of these

9. Which of the following makes the computer work when the electricity goes off?

(a) 

UPS

(b) 

Voltage

(c) 

Battery

(d) All of these

10. To shut down the computer, when you click the Start button, the .... box appears.

    (a) Close it   (b) Shut up

    (c) Shutdown   (d) None of these

11. Which is the first display screen when we switch on a computer?

Answer by looking at the picture.
(a) Taskbar   (b) Icon
(c) Desktop   (d) Monitor

12. Which one of the following of a CPU tower is pressed to restart the computer?
(a) Power Button   (b) Reset
(c) Both (a) and (b)   (d) Neither (a) nor (b)

13. What is the most important software on a computer?
(a) Video game software
(b) Microsoft Office software
(c) Operating System software
(d) Antivirus software

14. The correct procedure for shutting down a computer is
(i) .... on the start menu or icon
(ii) Click the .... icon
(iii) Click on .... from the options.
(a) switch // shut down // off
(b) turn // click // starts
(c) power//off//click
(d) click // power// shut down

15. Why is it important to focus your eyes away from the computer screen time to time?
(a) Typing reports on a computer is not recommended by most physicians.
(b) It helps rest your eyes and prevents eye strain.
(c) Computer screens cause leg pain.
(d) It lets you think about something else.

16. Arrange the below pictures in correct order of steps for turning on a computer.

I. 

II. 

III. 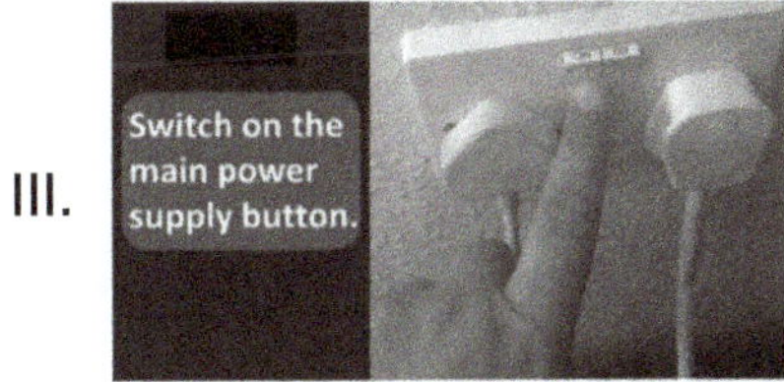

IV. 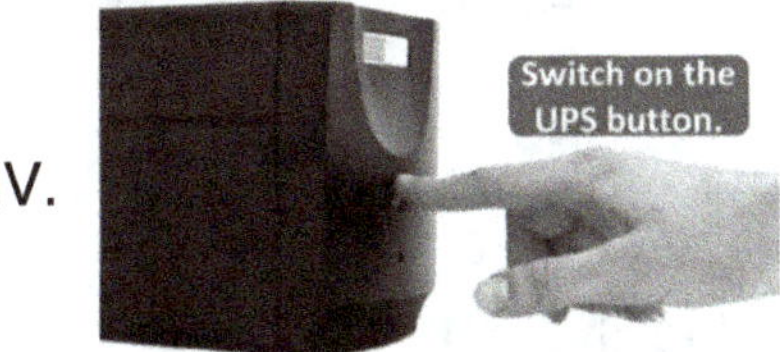

Codes

(a) IV, III, II, I

(b) II, III, IV, I

(c) I, II, III, IV

(d) III, IV, II, I

17. Which of the following pairs are correctly matched?

	List I	List II
(a)	When I finish using a computer, I do this.	Shutdown
(b)	I can do this if I type the correct user name and password.	Log out
(c)	A secret word Computer and I know.	Username
(d)	To turn off the computer I have to do this.	Log in

Darken your choice with HB Pencil

1.	(a) (b) (c) (d)	5.	(a) (b) (c) (d)	9.	(a) (b) (c) (d)	13.	(a) (b) (c) (d)	17.	(a) (b) (c) (d)
2.	(a) (b) (c) (d)	6.	(a) (b) (c) (d)	10.	(a) (b) (c) (d)	14.	(a) (b) (c) (d)		
3.	(a) (b) (c) (d)	7.	(a) (b) (c) (d)	11.	(a) (b) (c) (d)	15.	(a) (b) (c) (d)		
4.	(a) (b) (c) (d)	8.	(a) (b) (c) (d)	12.	(a) (b) (c) (d)	16.	(a) (b) (c) (d)		

Introduction to MS Paint 2016

1. Microsoft paint is a
   (a) Operating System
   (b) software
   (c) folder
   (d) All of these

2. This is present above the ribbon.
   It helps to do different functions with just one click. What is it?

   (a) Quick Access Toolbar
   (b) Ribbon
   (c) Drawing Area
   (d) Color Palette

3. The blank white area in which you can make your drawing and coloring is

   (a) Paper
   (b) Ribbon
   (c) Drawing area
   (d) Toolbar

4. For opening Paint program, after clicking the start button, we click on
   (a) My Computer   (b) MS Office
   (c) Paint   (d) All programs

5. For opening Paint program, which sequence we must follow?
   (a) Start, All programs, Accessories, Paint
   (b) All programs, Accessories, Paint, Start
   (c) Paint, All programs, Accessories, Start
   (d) All programs, Start, Accessories, Paint

6. What shapes do we use to draw the following image in MS Paint?

   (a) Oval   (b) Triangle and Oval
   (c) Oval and Rectangle   (d) Rectangle

7. What shape do you need to draw a Square?

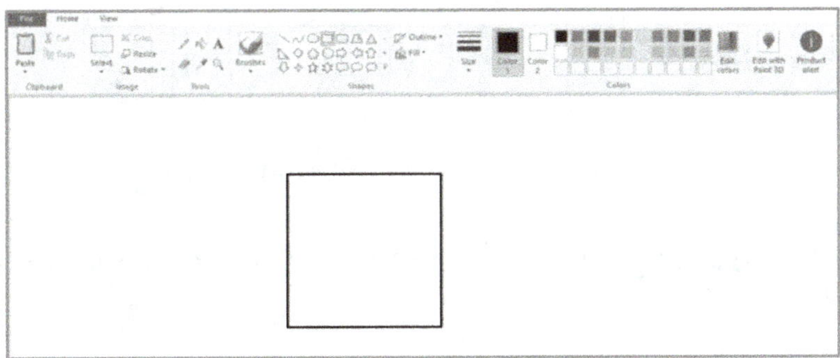

   (a) Oval   (b) Triangle
   (c) Star   (d) Rectangle

8. Look at this picture. I want to color the shape of the star. What tool will I use to color the shape?

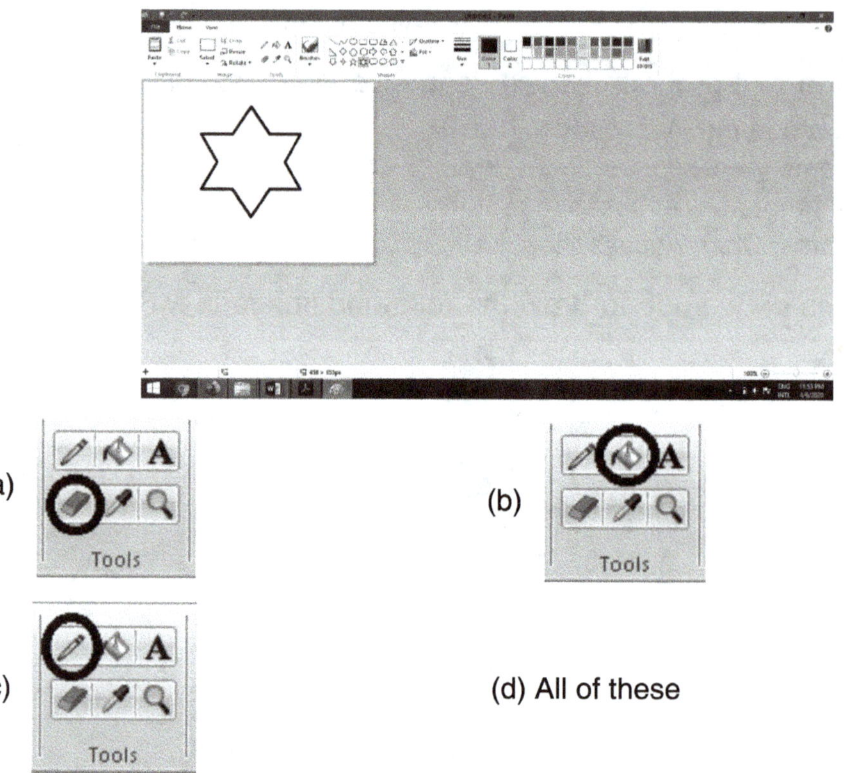

(a)  Tools   (b) Tools

(c) Tools   (d) All of these

9. Which of the following will you use to select any irregularly shaped part of the picture?

(a) Free-Form Select 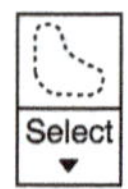   (b) Select 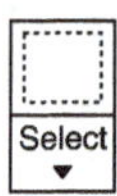

(c) Eraser    (d) Fill with color 

10. Which of the following will you use to fill the entire picture on an enclosed shape with color?

(a) 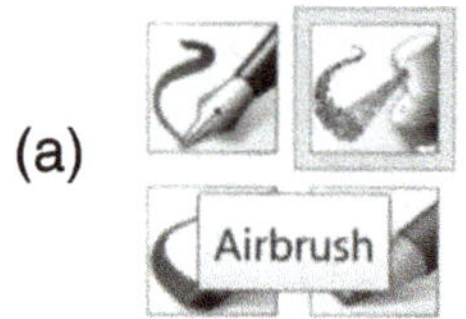   (b)    (c)    (d)

11. In MS Paint, what is the function of the tool shown below?

(a) Applies color to an image like spray paint or airbrush.
(b) Magnifies or zooms in on an area of an image.
(c) Erases a part of an image.
(d) Selects a free form (irregular-sized object).

12. Which is the tool used to draw thin, free-form lines or curves?

(a) 

(b) 

(c) 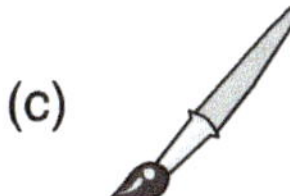

(d) 

13. Which of the following shows the Menu bar in Paint?

(a) 2   (b) 4
(c) 1   (d) 3

14. Which tool is this?

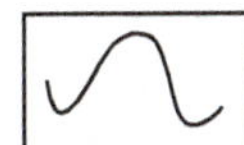

(a) Polygon   (b) Oval
(c) Curve   (d) Line

15. Which is a wrong match?

(a) 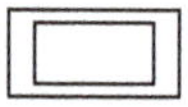 - Rectangle tool   (b) 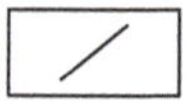 - Line tool

(c)  - Lasso tool   (d) 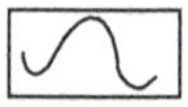 - Curve tool

16. To open MS Paint, we Select Start → [?   ] → All programs → Accessories → Paint program

(a) Open   (b) All apps

(c) Name   (d) Menu

17. In MS Paint Jack wants to write his name. Which tool is used to help him to write his name?

(a) 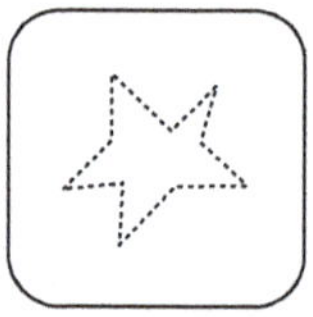   (b)

(c)    (d)

18. Which of the following are correctly matched?

	MS Paint Tools	Name
1.	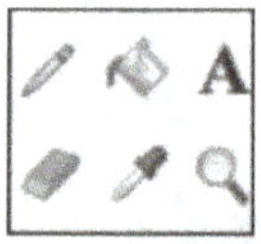	Tools group
2.	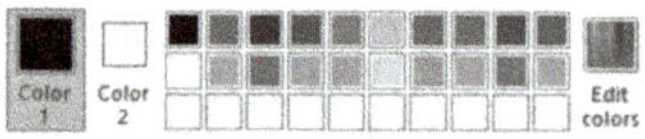	Shapes group
3.	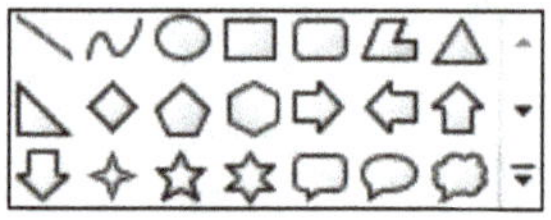	Colors group

(a) Only 1   (b) 1 and 2

(c) Only 2   (d) 2 and 3

19. Identify the incorrect statement about MS Paint from the following.

   (a) To save a file in paint, click on file button, then save option and then save by giving the file a suitable name.

   (b) There are only a few tools used in MS paint such as a pencil, eraser, magnifier and brushes.

   (c) We can magnify a picture in MS paint using magnifier tool.

   (d) To open a new drawing area in MS paint, click on paint and then the new option.

20. Which one of the following statements is/are true?

   (a) MS Paint application has magnification tool.

   (b) MS Paint application has eraser tool.

   (c) MS Paint application has ellipse tool.

   (d) All of the above

Darken your choice with HB Pencil

1.	ⓐ ⓑ ⓒ ⓓ	**5.**	ⓐ ⓑ ⓒ ⓓ	**9.**	ⓐ ⓑ ⓒ ⓓ	**13.**	ⓐ ⓑ ⓒ ⓓ	**17.**	ⓐ ⓑ ⓒ ⓓ
2.	ⓐ ⓑ ⓒ ⓓ	**6.**	ⓐ ⓑ ⓒ ⓓ	**10.**	ⓐ ⓑ ⓒ ⓓ	**14.**	ⓐ ⓑ ⓒ ⓓ	**18.**	ⓐ ⓑ ⓒ ⓓ
3.	ⓐ ⓑ ⓒ ⓓ	**7.**	ⓐ ⓑ ⓒ ⓓ	**11.**	ⓐ ⓑ ⓒ ⓓ	**15.**	ⓐ ⓑ ⓒ ⓓ	**19.**	ⓐ ⓑ ⓒ ⓓ
4.	ⓐ ⓑ ⓒ ⓓ	**8.**	ⓐ ⓑ ⓒ ⓓ	**12.**	ⓐ ⓑ ⓒ ⓓ	**16.**	ⓐ ⓑ ⓒ ⓓ	**20.**	ⓐ ⓑ ⓒ ⓓ

08

Latest Developments in the Field of IT

1. You can watch videos with me and I have a red and white logo! What app am I?

   (a) Google Chrome   (b) WhatsApp

   (c) Facebook   (d) YouTube

2. While playing a racing game, which keys combination is more commonly used for moving the bike?

   (a) Function keys   (b) Numeric keys

   (c) Arrow keys   (d) All of these

3. I am useful for recording songs. Who am I?

   (a) Speakers   (b) Microphone

   (c) CPU   (d) Mouse

4. These devices are used to send voice messages and to communicate. One common term used with them is "over and out". Identify the devices.

(a) 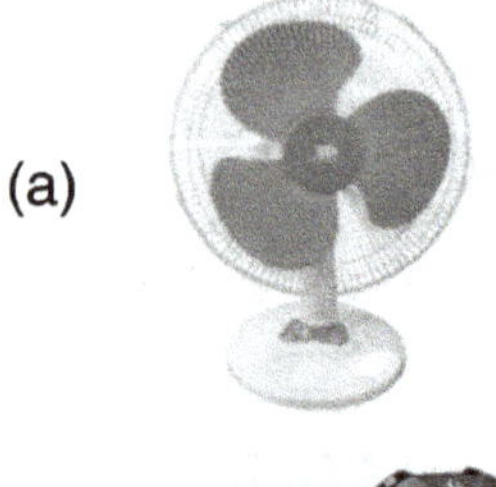
         (b) 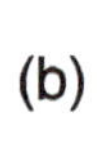 

(c) 
         (d) 

5. Which of these could protect your computer data?
   (a) Locking your computer away.
   (b) Installing an anti-virus software.
   (c) Only using computers during the day.
   (d) Cleaning your computer with clean cloth.

6. What does the given image represent?

   (a) Hardware   (b) Game
   (c) Music file   (d) Antivirus

7. Which of the following is not used to send information through internet?
   (a) Facebook   (b) Microsoft Word
   (c) Zoom   (d) WhatsApp

8. A computer virus can spread through
   (a) E-mails   (b) pen drives
   (c) Both (a) and (b)   (d) None of these

9. The USERNAME is
   (a) a code that tells the computer who you are.
   (b) a secret code used to keep your computer safe.
   (c) the second step in the log in process.
   (d) a list of folders, files and programs on your computer.

10. Which computer program converts Assembly Language to Machine language?
    (a) Interpreter   (b) Compiler
    (c) Assembler   (d) Comparator

11. Mac Operating System is developed by which company?

   (a) IBM   (b) Microsoft

   (c) Samsung   (d) Apple

12. A programmer create computer virus not

   (a) to take money   (b) to steal sensitive data

   (c) to disable computer   (d) to infect computer

13. Google Docs is Google's version of

   (a) Microsoft Word   (b) Microsoft Excel

   (c) Microsoft Outlook   (d) Microsoft Publisher

14. Identify the following device which can also do some tasks of smartphone.

   (a) Intelligent-wrist   (b) Smart watch

   (c) Smart wrist   (d) Smart hand

Darken your choice with HB Pencil

1.	ⓐ ⓑ ⓒ ⓓ	5.	ⓐ ⓑ ⓒ ⓓ	9.	ⓐ ⓑ ⓒ ⓓ	13.	ⓐ ⓑ ⓒ ⓓ
2.	ⓐ ⓑ ⓒ ⓓ	6.	ⓐ ⓑ ⓒ ⓓ	10.	ⓐ ⓑ ⓒ ⓓ	14.	ⓐ ⓑ ⓒ ⓓ
3.	ⓐ ⓑ ⓒ ⓓ	7.	ⓐ ⓑ ⓒ ⓓ	11.	ⓐ ⓑ ⓒ ⓓ		
4.	ⓐ ⓑ ⓒ ⓓ	8.	ⓐ ⓑ ⓒ ⓓ	12.	ⓐ ⓑ ⓒ ⓓ		

Practice Sets

1-3

Practice Set 01

Time : 60 Mins.   Max. Marks : 35

General Instructions
1. This question paper contains 35 questions.
2. All questions are compulsory. There is no negative marking.
3. Use HB pencil / Blue ball point pen to mark your choice of answer by darkening the circles on the OMR Sheet.

1. Which of the following tools is not used while drawing the given picture?

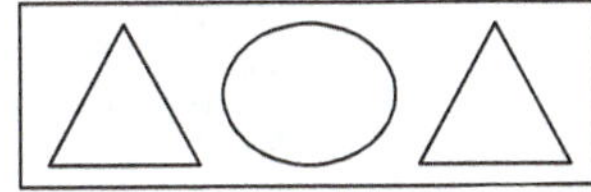

   (a) Oval tool   (b) Rectangle tool
   (c) Pencil tool   (d) Line tool

2. Steve has a DVD of a new movie. He wants to watch this movie. Is it possible for him to watch the movie on the computer?
   (a) Yes   (b) No
   (c) Possibility is less   (d) Possibility is more

3. With the help of a given type of machine, you can

   (a) listen to music   (b) eat food
   (c) clean house   (d) plant trees

4. Which of the following is not a type of computer?
   (a) Laptop   (b) Tablet
   (c) Palmtop   (d) Tabtop

5. Select the correct match.

(a)  Laptop

(b)  Mobile phone

(c) 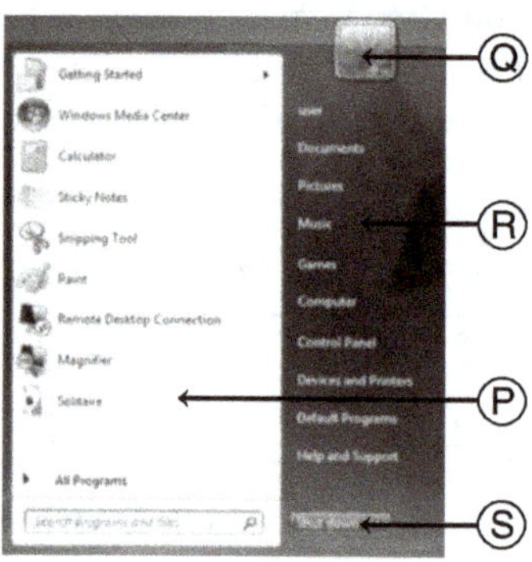 Tablet computer

(d) Desktop computer

6. Which of the following portions of the start menu will you click to shut down the computer?

(a) P

(b) Q

(c) R

(d) S

7. After switching on the UPS, which part of the computer is powered on?

(a) 

(b) 

(c) 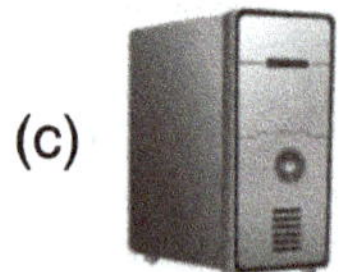

(d) 

8. With the help of which part of the computer, the Shut down option is selected in the start menu?

(a) 

(b) 

(c) 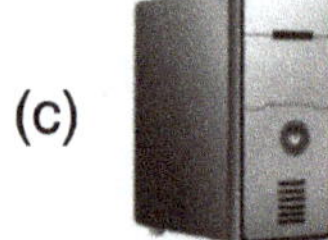

(d) 

9. Which of the following parts is used to keep the computer on, when there is a power failure?

    (a) Monitor   (b) Keyboard

    (c) Mouse   (d) UPS

10. Which of the following options safely Shut down the computer and then start it again?

    (a) Log off   (b) Shut down

    (c) Restart   (d) Sleep

11. The buttons present on a keyboard are called

    (a) wheels   (b) keys

    (c) scrolls   (d) printers

12. Words and sentences are typed using .... keys.

    (a) number   (b) special

    (c) alphabet   (d) control

13. Whatever is typed on keyboard, it can be seen on the

    (a) printer   (b) CPU

    (c) monitor   (d) speaker

14. Select the incorrect match.

    (a) ↑ Moves the cursor up.

    (b) ↓ Moves the cursor down.

    (c) → Moves the cursor to the right.

    (d) Enter Moves the cursor to the left.

15. To type capital letters, turn on the .... key on the keyboard.

    (a) Delete   (b) Enter

    (c) Caps Lock   (d) Arrow

16. Mouse is connected to

    (a) CPU   (b) UPS

    (c) keyboard   (d) monitor

17. A .... keeps the mouse free from dust and dirt.

(a) mouse pad   (b) rubber pad

(c) paper pad   (d) All of these

18. Which finger is placed on the left mouse button?

(a) Middle   (b) Index

(c) Little   (d) Thumb

19. .... clicking the mouse opens an item on the computer.

(a) Single   (b) Double

(c) Triple   (d) None of these

20. Which of the following mouse actions displays a list of commands on screen?

(a) Right click   (b) Drag and drop

(c) Scrolling   (d) Left click

21. Which of the following tasks of a TV can be performed by computer?

(a) Playing movies   (b) Playing music

(c) Managing volume   (d) All of these

22. Select the correct statement.

(a) Songs can be played using a computer.

(b) A computer cannot be used to solve sums.

(c) We cannot make drawing on the computer.

(d) We cannot play games on a computer.

23. In hospitals, computers are used to

(a) store data about patients

(b) to sell tickets

(c) to record TV shows

(d) to monitor flight timings

24. Which of the following games can be played on a computer?

(a) Racing   (b) Cricket

(c) Basketball   (d) All of these

25. Which one of the following is the CPU?

(a) 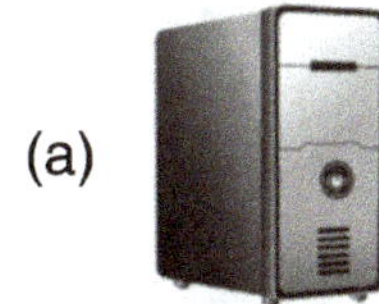

(b) 

(c) 

(d) None of these

26. Jack wants to write his name on the computer. Which part of the computer helps him write his name?

(a) Monitor

(b) CPU

(c) Mouse

(d) Keyboard

27. Which of the following statements is/are correct?

I. Computer is not a machine.

II. Computer is a machine.

Codes

(a) Only I

(b) Only II

(c) Both I and II

(d) None of these

28. How many letters of alphabet are there on the keyboard?

(a) 15

(b) 20

(c) 25

(d) 26

29. Arrange the following machines in a largest to smallest order, regarding the amount of space they take on a table.

I. 

II. 

III. 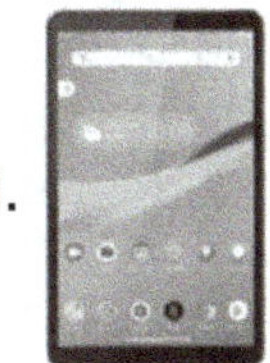

Codes

(a) I-II-III

(b) II-III-I

(c) III-II-I

(d) I-III-II

30. Which of the following tools is used in the given image?

(A)   (B)

(C)   (D) All of these

31. Which of the following option uses very little power, i.e. the computer enters a low-power state?

(a) Log Off   (b) Shut down

(c) Sleep   (d) Restart

32. Which of the following tools is used in drawing the given shape?

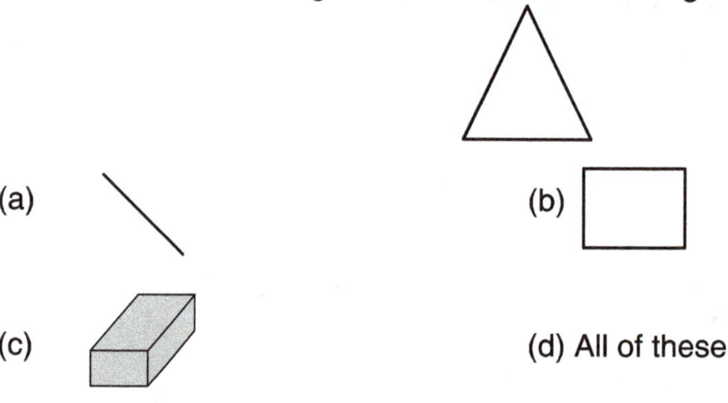

(a)   (b)

(c)   (d) All of these

33. Identify the following.

  I. It is an electronic machine that never gets tired.

II. You can play games on it.

Codes

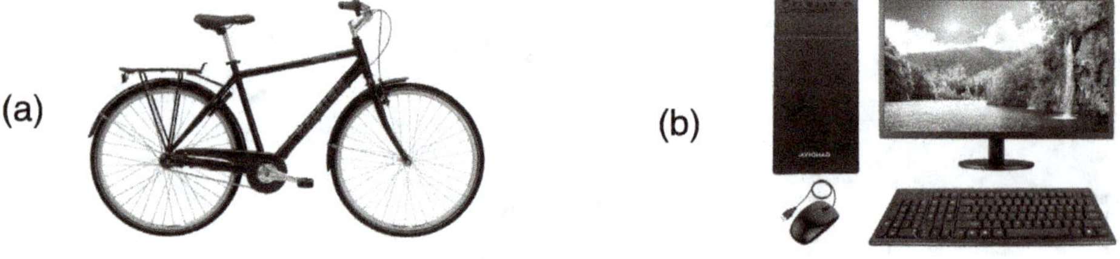

(a)   (b)

(c)

(d)

34. Which among the following is not a wearable computer?

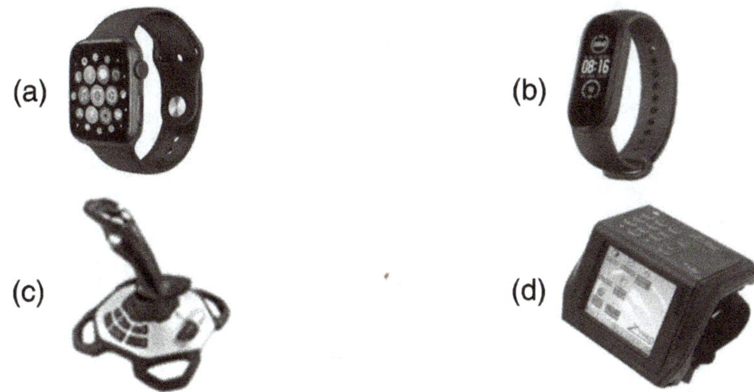

(a)

(b)

(c)

(d)

35. Identify the given device.

I. You can carry it wherever you go, as they are small in size and can fit in your pockets.

II. It has a touchscreen as its display screen.

Codes

(a) Laptop

(b) Desktop computer

(c) Smartphones

(d) None of these

Darken your choice with HB Pencil

1. ⓐ ⓑ ⓒ ⓓ	7. ⓐ ⓑ ⓒ ⓓ	13. ⓐ ⓑ ⓒ ⓓ	19. ⓐ ⓑ ⓒ ⓓ	25. ⓐ ⓑ ⓒ ⓓ	31. ⓐ ⓑ ⓒ ⓓ
2. ⓐ ⓑ ⓒ ⓓ	8. ⓐ ⓑ ⓒ ⓓ	14. ⓐ ⓑ ⓒ ⓓ	20. ⓐ ⓑ ⓒ ⓓ	26. ⓐ ⓑ ⓒ ⓓ	32. ⓐ ⓑ ⓒ ⓓ
3. ⓐ ⓑ ⓒ ⓓ	9. ⓐ ⓑ ⓒ ⓓ	15. ⓐ ⓑ ⓒ ⓓ	21. ⓐ ⓑ ⓒ ⓓ	27. ⓐ ⓑ ⓒ ⓓ	33. ⓐ ⓑ ⓒ ⓓ
4. ⓐ ⓑ ⓒ ⓓ	10. ⓐ ⓑ ⓒ ⓓ	16. ⓐ ⓑ ⓒ ⓓ	22. ⓐ ⓑ ⓒ ⓓ	28. ⓐ ⓑ ⓒ ⓓ	34. ⓐ ⓑ ⓒ ⓓ
5. ⓐ ⓑ ⓒ ⓓ	11. ⓐ ⓑ ⓒ ⓓ	17. ⓐ ⓑ ⓒ ⓓ	23. ⓐ ⓑ ⓒ ⓓ	29. ⓐ ⓑ ⓒ ⓓ	35. ⓐ ⓑ ⓒ ⓓ
6. ⓐ ⓑ ⓒ ⓓ	12. ⓐ ⓑ ⓒ ⓓ	18. ⓐ ⓑ ⓒ ⓓ	24. ⓐ ⓑ ⓒ ⓓ	30. ⓐ ⓑ ⓒ ⓓ	

Practice Set 02

General Instructions

1. This question paper contains 35 questions.
2. All questions are compulsory. There is no negative marking.
3. Use HB pencil / Blue ball point pen to mark your choice of answer by darkening the circles on the OMR Sheet.

1. Computer is known as a smart machine, because
    (a) it does not make mistake on its own.
    (b) it never gets tired.
    (c) it works very fast.
    (d) All of the above

2. We see different types of 'Apps' in our smartphone. What does the word 'App' mean?
    (a) Applicant
    (b) Application
    (c) Apply
    (d) Applicate

3. Which of the following statements is correct about the given device?

    (a) It is a type of computer.
    (b) It can be carried from one place to another.
    (c) It is called a laptop.
    (d) All of the above

4. Select the correct statement about the jumbled word given below.
   CMOUPETR

   (a) It is a man-made machine.   (b) It is not an electronic machine.

   (c) You cannot play music on it.   (d) You cannot solve sums on it.

5. Which of the following types of computers can be used to play games?

   (a)    (b) 

   (c) 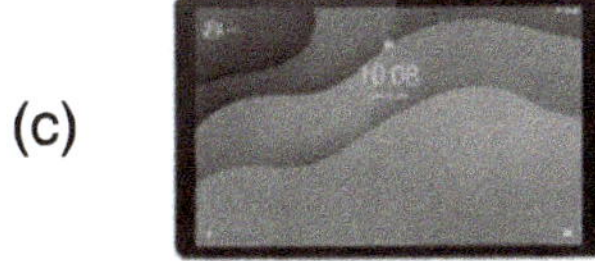   (d) All of these

6. The small pictures marked as (P) in the given image that we see on the desktop are called

   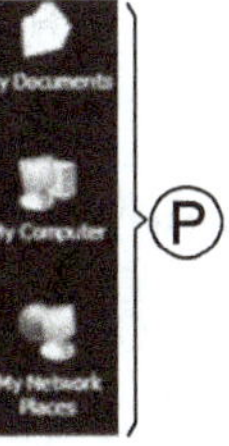

   (a) icons   (b) pins
   (c) snaps   (d) clips

7. When a computer is not in use
   (a) it must be covered properly.
   (b) it must be cleaned with a wet cloth.
   (c) its wires should be detached.
   (d) we can play with its parts.

8. The sequence of actions done by the computer to get everything ready for use, while starting is called
   (a) tapping   (b) logging
   (c) booting   (d) clicking

9. To start a laptop, you just need to

   (a) press power button available on the laptop.

   (b) press the ⊞ key.

   (c) tap twice on touchpad.

   (d) press the Spacebar.

10. A computer is switched off, when it is not in use to

   (a) supply power to its parts   (b) save electricity

   (c) keep it warm   (d) increase its speed

11. Which key can be used to type a letter in capital when Caps Lock key is OFF?

   (a) Ctrl   (b) alt

   (c) Shift   (d) Enter

12. .... key is also called the return key.

   (a) Space bar   (b) Enter

   (c) Delete   (d) Backspace

13. Which of the following words cannot be completed with the given set of keys?

   E   A   P   H   O   F   C

   (a) S __ I __ T   (b) C A __ S L __ __ K

   (c) S __ A C __ B __ R   (d) D E __ E __ E

14. Observe the position of the cursor in the given snapshot.

   RIG|HT ← Cursor

   Re-arrange the steps given below to replace letter R with letter T.

   I. Press T key

   II. Press ← key two times

   III. Press Backspace key

   Codes

   (a) I-II-III   (b) II-I-III

   (c) I-III-II   (d) II-III-I

15. What is the difference between ⌈Delete⌉ key and ⌈←Backspace⌉ key?

    (a) Delete key is used to erase character, backspace key is used to give a small gap between two characters.

    (b) Delete key erases characters to the right of the cursor. Backspace key erases character to the left of the cursor one character at a time.

    (c) Delete key erase character to the left of cursor. Backspace key erases characters to the right of the cursor.

    (d) All of the above

16. Which of the following statements is/are correct about mouse?

    (a) It is a hand-operated device.

    (b) It sits outside the computer case.

    (c) It comes in many shapes and sizes.

    (d) All of the above

17. A wireless mouse

    (a) connects with the computer with a cable

    (b) does not have a cable

    (c) is not required to click

    (d) is tough to operate

18. Which of the following pairs are incorrectly matched?

    (a) Click and drag — Pressing and holding the mouse button and moving.

    (b) Double - Click — Moving the mouse wheel up or down.

    (c) Scrolling — Pressing the mouse button twice.

    (d) Both (b) and (c)

19. You will see the menu as shown in the given image when you .... the mouse.

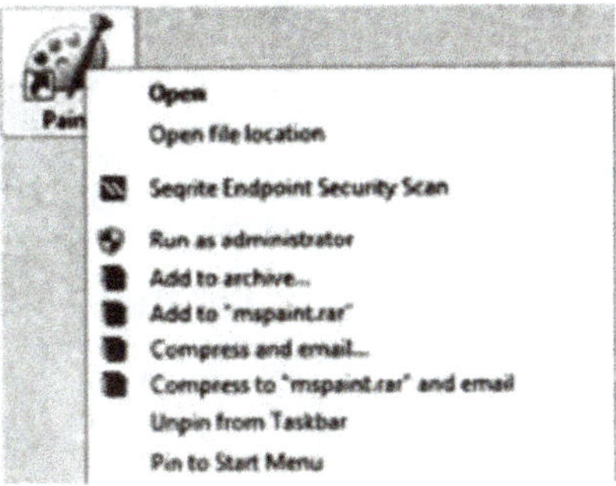

(a) drag   (b) wiggle

(c) double - click   (d) right - click

20. A computer mouse helps us to move the .... from one place to another.

(a) cursor   (b) printer

(c) icon   (d) pointer

21. What is the function of the mouse of a computer?

(a) It is used to write something.

(b) It is used to move the pointer on the computer screen.

(c) It is used to display something.

(d) All of the above

22. We switch off computer when not in use to

(a) supply power to its parts   (b) save electricity

(c) increase its speed   (d) keep it cool

23. A .... is used for printing text and pictures from a computer on to paper.

(a) scanner   (b) printer

(c) speaker   (d) CPU

24. Which of the following statements is correct about the term 'App'?

(a) It is a small program found in mobile device.

(b) It is a program found in joy stick.

(c) It is a program that erases all the other programs of the computer.

(d) It is a oval tool in the MS Paint.

25. There are .... types of keys on a keyboard.

(a) 1   (b) 2

(c) 5   (d) 4

26. Which of the following tools help you to draw the free-form lines?

(a)   (b)

(c)   (d) Both (a) and (b)

27. The given set of tools and shapes are found in

    (a) toolbox   (b) workspace area
    (c) ribbon   (d) All of these

28. Which of the following tools is used to draw the closed shapes?

    (a) □   (b) ○

    (c)    (d) Both (a) and (b)

29. Identify the following.
    You can use it to draw the free-hand drawing.
    By using this tool, you can even draw perfect straight line, while holding
    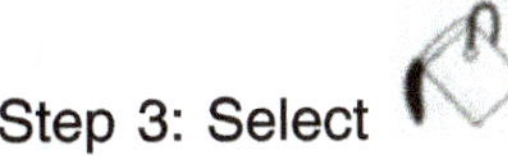 key.

    (a)    (b) ✏

    (c) □   (d) ○

30. What would be the result of the given steps?
        Step 1: Select an Oval tool.
        Step 2: Go to drawing area, click and drag the mouse to draw an oval shape.

        Step 3: Select 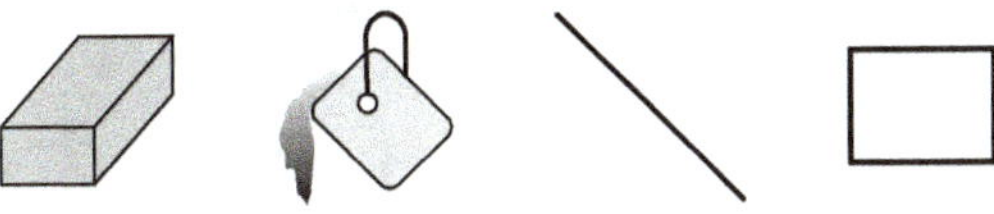
        Step 4: Select any color from the color palette.
        Step 5: Go to the oval shape, and right click the mouse.

(a) 

(b)

(c)

(d)

31. Which of the following is an app?

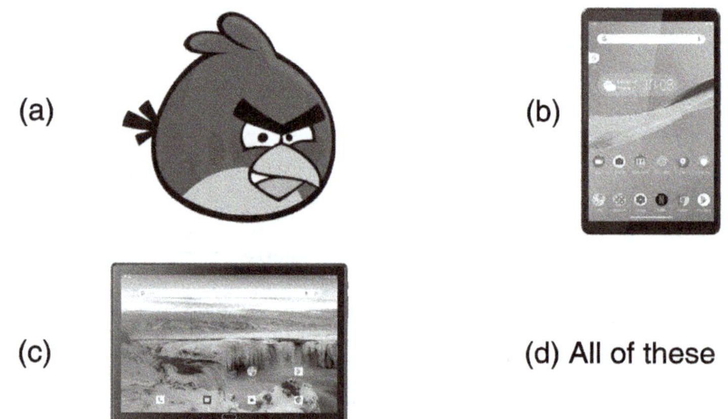

(a)

(b)

(c)

(d) All of these

32. Wearable computers are the devices that can do all the tasks, performed by a .... .You can wear them on the body.

(a) smartphone   (b) app

(c) application   (d) None of these

33. Which of the following is a wearable computer?

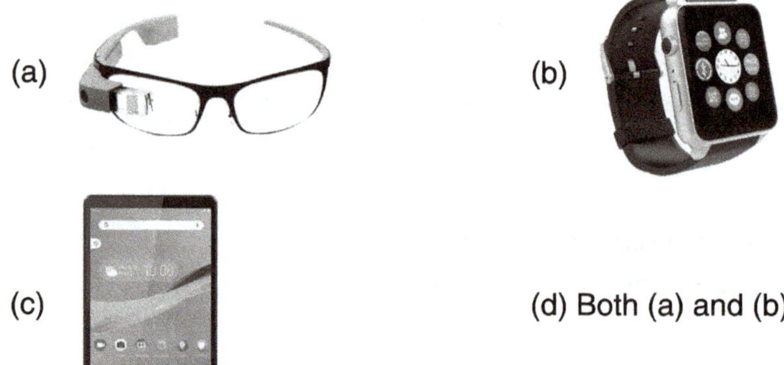

(a)

(b)

(c)

(d) Both (a) and (b)

34. .... is the brain of a computer.

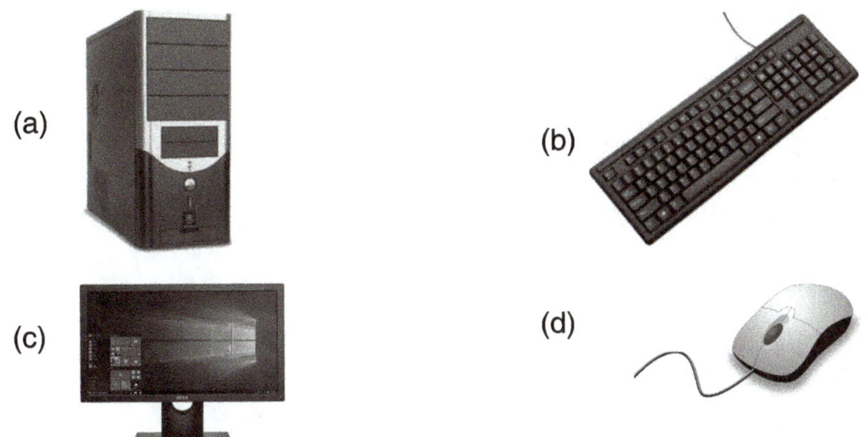

(a)

(b)

(c)

(d)

35. Which of the following games can be played on a smartphone?

(a)

(b)

(c)

(d) All of these

Darken your choice with HB Pencil

1.	ⓐ ⓑ ⓒ ⓓ	7.	ⓐ ⓑ ⓒ ⓓ	13.	ⓐ ⓑ ⓒ ⓓ	19.	ⓐ ⓑ ⓒ ⓓ	25.	ⓐ ⓑ ⓒ ⓓ	31.	ⓐ ⓑ ⓒ ⓓ
2.	ⓐ ⓑ ⓒ ⓓ	8.	ⓐ ⓑ ⓒ ⓓ	14.	ⓐ ⓑ ⓒ ⓓ	20.	ⓐ ⓑ ⓒ ⓓ	26.	ⓐ ⓑ ⓒ ⓓ	32.	ⓐ ⓑ ⓒ ⓓ
3.	ⓐ ⓑ ⓒ ⓓ	9.	ⓐ ⓑ ⓒ ⓓ	15.	ⓐ ⓑ ⓒ ⓓ	21.	ⓐ ⓑ ⓒ ⓓ	27.	ⓐ ⓑ ⓒ ⓓ	33.	ⓐ ⓑ ⓒ ⓓ
4.	ⓐ ⓑ ⓒ ⓓ	10.	ⓐ ⓑ ⓒ ⓓ	16.	ⓐ ⓑ ⓒ ⓓ	22.	ⓐ ⓑ ⓒ ⓓ	28.	ⓐ ⓑ ⓒ ⓓ	34.	ⓐ ⓑ ⓒ ⓓ
5.	ⓐ ⓑ ⓒ ⓓ	11.	ⓐ ⓑ ⓒ ⓓ	17.	ⓐ ⓑ ⓒ ⓓ	23.	ⓐ ⓑ ⓒ ⓓ	29.	ⓐ ⓑ ⓒ ⓓ	35.	ⓐ ⓑ ⓒ ⓓ
6.	ⓐ ⓑ ⓒ ⓓ	12.	ⓐ ⓑ ⓒ ⓓ	18.	ⓐ ⓑ ⓒ ⓓ	24.	ⓐ ⓑ ⓒ ⓓ	30.	ⓐ ⓑ ⓒ ⓓ		

Practice Set 03

Time : 60 Mins.   Max. Marks : 35

General Instructions
1. This question paper contains 35 questions.
2. All questions are compulsory. There is no negative marking.
3. Use HB pencil / Blue ball point pen to mark your choice of answer by darkening the circles on the OMR Sheet.

1. What does the CPU stand for?
   (a) Control Processing Unit
   (b) Call Processing Unit
   (c) Central Processing Unit
   (d) Copy Processing Unit

2. What does a Printer do?
   (a) Display images and text
   (b) Play audio and video
   (c) Print images and text on paper
   (d) Produce sound for audio

3. Which of these devices is responsible for displaying output in a computer?
   (a) CD ROM
   (b) Monitor
   (c) Speakers
   (d) Keyboard

4. When was the first computer invented?
   (a) 1834
   (b) 1827
   (c) 1822
   (d) 1945

5. Which of these computer devices runs on a battery?
   (a) Desktop computer
   (b) Laptop
   (c) Tablet
   (d) Both (b) and (c)

6. Unscramble the given word and select the statement which is correct about it.

   BOOIGNT

   (a) It is performed when computer is switched off.
   (b) It is the first step performed to start a computer.
   (c) It is performed when the computer starts.
   (d) It is the last step performed to shut down a computer.

7. Unscramble the given words and identify which of the following are incorrectly matched?

    (a) GOINL – End access to a computer system.

    (b) WODARPSS – Gaining access to use computer.

    (c) TOGUOL – Secret combination of letters and number.

    (d) All of the above

8. We use .... and .... to get access to the computer.

    (a) username, password   (b) password, web name

    (c) web name, crossword   (d) crossword, last name

9. Choose the incorrect regarding the order to start a computer.

    (a) Switch on the CPU.   (b) Switch off the monitor.

    (c) Switch on the UPS.   (d) Switch on the power switch.

10. How can you keep your computer dust free?

    (a) By washing it with water   (b) By blowing air on it

    (c) By cleaning it with a dry cloth   (d) Both (a) and (b)

11. Which of the following statements is incorrect about alphabet keys?

    (a) They are used for typing letters and words.

    (b) There are 26 alphabet keys on the keyboard.

    (c) The first six letters of alphabet keys form the name of a keyboard layout.

    (d) The last seven letters of the alphabet keys form the name of the inventor of the keyboard.

12. Identify the following.

    It is a watch that you can wear on your wrist.

    It can perform all the tasks, done by a smart phone.

    (a) Smart watch   (b) Intelligent-wrist

    (c) Smart wrist   (d) Smart band

13. Caps lock is also called as .... key.
(a) toggle   (b) return
(c) symbol   (d) extra

14. Which of the following keys would you use to type your name and age?
(a) Number keys   (b) Alphabet keys
(c) Arrow keys   (d) Both (a) and (b)

15. How many F(function) keys are there on a keyboard ?
(a) 10   (b) 12
(c) 15   (d) 20

16. .... allows us to interact with smartphone with our fingers.
(a) Dual screen   (b) Pick screen
(c) Touch screen   (d) Smart screen

17. Which of the following statements is/are correct regarding mouse?
   I. Small finger is placed on the left mouse button.
   II. A mouse is always kept on a rough surface.
   III. It is used for moving items on screen.
   Codes
(a) Only I   (b) Only II
(c) Only III   (d) All of these

18. A mouse is a/an
(a) input device   (b) output device
(c) processing device   (d) All of these

19. Computer mouse is a part of
(a) motherboard   (b) keyboard
(c) hardware   (d) software

20. Which one is not part of computer mouse?
(a) Left button   (b) Scroll wheel
(c) Monitor   (d) Connecting wire

21. In which of the following areas computers are not used for education?
    (a) Schools   (b) Colleges
    (c) Homes   (d) Banks

22. Which of the following tools is found in the Toolbox in MS Paint?
    (a) 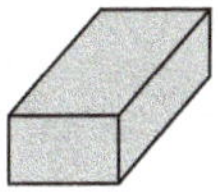   (b)

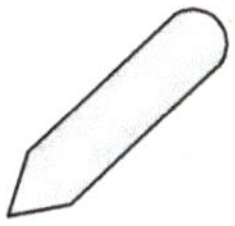

    (c)    (d) All of these

23. Select the word which when unscrambled gives the name of a place, where computers are used.
    (a) SMUS   (b) VOLSE
    (c) NABK   (d) POME

24. Which of the following is a gaming device?
    (a)    (b)

    (c)    (d) All of these

25. Select the incorrect match regarding the uses of the computer.
    (a) Offices - Maintaining employee records
    (b) Schools - Diagnosing diseases
    (c) Banks - Money withdrawal through ATM
    (d) Railways - Booking Tickets

26. Which of the following is another name for the CPU of a computer ?

    (a) A RAM

    (b) A microprocessor

    (c) A sound card

    (d) A video graphics card

27. A .... is used for printing text and pictures from a computer onto paper.

    (a) scanner   (b) printer

    (c) speaker   (d) CPU

28. Which of these are physical devices that a computer can use?

    (a) Hardware   (b) Software

    (c) System Software   (d) Package

29. Where is data stored in a computer?

    (a) Monitor   (b) Keyboard

    (c) CPU   (d) Mouse

30. What is the full form of RAM?

    (a) Reliability, Availability and Maintainability

    (b) Rarely Adequate Memory

    (c) Raised Angle Marker

    (d) Random Access Memory

31. Which of the following tools is not used in drawing the given picture?

(a) 

(b)

(c)

(d)

32. What is the drawing area?
    (a) It is an area where you can draw shapes and pictures.
    (b) It is an area where you can choose colors and shapes for the drawing.
    (c) It is an area where tools are found.
    (d) None of the above

33. Which of the following tools fill the given shapes with colors?

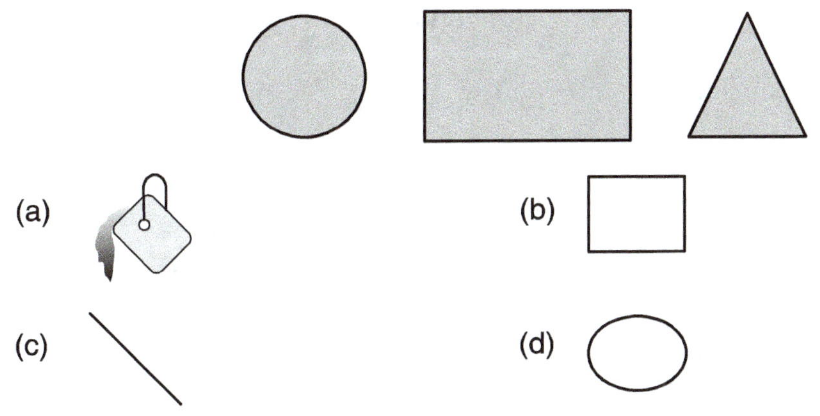

(a)

(b)

(c)

(d)

34. What is the following tool called?

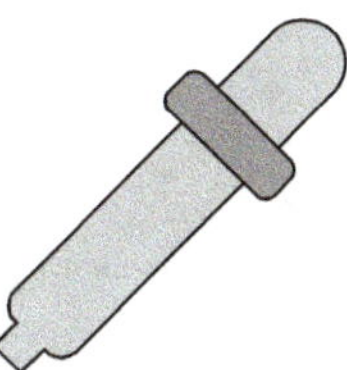

(a) Color picker   (b) Fill color
(c) Pencil   (d) Brush

35. Which of the following types of computers can be used while travelling?

I. 

II. 

III. 

Codes

(a) Only I

(b) II and III

(c) Only III

(d) I and III

1.	ⓐ ⓑ ⓒ ⓓ	7.	ⓐ ⓑ ⓒ ⓓ	13.	ⓐ ⓑ ⓒ ⓓ	19.	ⓐ ⓑ ⓒ ⓓ	25.	ⓐ ⓑ ⓒ ⓓ	31.	ⓐ ⓑ ⓒ ⓓ
2.	ⓐ ⓑ ⓒ ⓓ	8.	ⓐ ⓑ ⓒ ⓓ	14.	ⓐ ⓑ ⓒ ⓓ	20.	ⓐ ⓑ ⓒ ⓓ	26.	ⓐ ⓑ ⓒ ⓓ	32.	ⓐ ⓑ ⓒ ⓓ
3.	ⓐ ⓑ ⓒ ⓓ	9.	ⓐ ⓑ ⓒ ⓓ	15.	ⓐ ⓑ ⓒ ⓓ	21.	ⓐ ⓑ ⓒ ⓓ	27.	ⓐ ⓑ ⓒ ⓓ	33.	ⓐ ⓑ ⓒ ⓓ
4.	ⓐ ⓑ ⓒ ⓓ	10.	ⓐ ⓑ ⓒ ⓓ	16.	ⓐ ⓑ ⓒ ⓓ	22.	ⓐ ⓑ ⓒ ⓓ	28.	ⓐ ⓑ ⓒ ⓓ	34.	ⓐ ⓑ ⓒ ⓓ
5.	ⓐ ⓑ ⓒ ⓓ	11.	ⓐ ⓑ ⓒ ⓓ	17.	ⓐ ⓑ ⓒ ⓓ	23.	ⓐ ⓑ ⓒ ⓓ	29.	ⓐ ⓑ ⓒ ⓓ	35.	ⓐ ⓑ ⓒ ⓓ
6.	ⓐ ⓑ ⓒ ⓓ	12.	ⓐ ⓑ ⓒ ⓓ	18.	ⓐ ⓑ ⓒ ⓓ	24.	ⓐ ⓑ ⓒ ⓓ	30.	ⓐ ⓑ ⓒ ⓓ		

Answer Sheet

Chapter 1

1. (c)	2. (a)	3. (b)	4. (a)	5. (b)	6. (c)	7. (b)	8. (b)	9. (b)	10. (c)
11. (c)	12. (c)	13. (c)	14. (d)	15. (c)	16. (c)				

Chapter 2

1. (b)	2. (a)	3. (a)	4. (c)	5. (a)	6. (d)	7. (a)	8. (c)	9. (c)	10. (b)
11. (b)	12. (b)	13. (c)	14. (c)	15. (a)	16. (d)	17. (d)	18. (a)	19. (c)	20. (a)
21. (a)									

Chapter 3

1. (c)	2. (b)	3. (a)	4. (d)	5. (b)	6. (c)	7. (c)	8. (b)	9. (b)	10. (d)
11. (a)	12. (c)	13. (c)							

Chapter 4

1. (b)	2. (b)	3. (c)	4. (b)	5. (b)	6. (a)	7. (b)	8. (d)	9. (c)	10. (a)
11. (c)	12. (b)	13. (a)	14. (a)	15. (c)	16. (a)				

Chapter 5

1. (d)	2. (c)	3. (b)	4. (c)	5. (a)	6. (c)	7. (b)	8. (a)	9. (d)	10. (c)
11. (b)	12. (c)	13. (b)	14. (b)	15. (d)	16. (b)	17. (d)			

Chapter 6

1. (b)	2. (b)	3. (c)	4. (a)	5. (c)	6. (d)	7. (c)	8. (b)	9. (a)	10. (c)
11. (c)	12. (a)	13. (c)	14. (d)	15. (b)	16. (d)	17. (a)			

Chapter 7

1. (b)	2. (a)	3. (c)	4. (d)	5. (a)	6. (c)	7. (d)	8. (b)	9. (a)	10. (b)
11. (b)	12. (a)	13. (a)	14. (c)	15. (c)	16. (d)	17. (d)	18. (a)	19. (b)	20. (d)

Chapter 8

1. (d)	2. (c)	3. (b)	4. (b)	5. (b)	6. (b)	7. (b)	8. (c)	9. (a)	10. (c)
11. (d)	12. (c)	13. (a)	14. (b)						

Practice Set 1

1. (c)	2. (a)	3. (a)	4. (d)	5. (c)	6. (d)	7. (c)	8. (a)	9. (d)	10. (c)
11. (b)	12. (c)	13. (c)	14. (d)	15. (c)	16. (a)	17. (a)	18. (b)	19. (b)	20. (a)
21. (d)	22. (a)	23. (a)	24. (d)	25. (a)	26. (d)	27. (b)	28. (d)	29. (a)	30. (b)
31. (c)	32. (a)	33. (b)	34. (c)	35. (c)					

Practice Set 2

1. (d)	2. (b)	3. (d)	4. (a)	5. (d)	6. (a)	7. (a)	8. (c)	9. (a)	10. (b)
11. (c)	12. (b)	13. (d)	14. (d)	15. (b)	16. (d)	17. (b)	18. (d)	19. (d)	20. (d)
21. (b)	22. (b)	23. (b)	24. (a)	25. (c)	26. (a)	27. (a)	28. (d)	29. (b)	30. (a)
31. (a)	32. (a)	33. (d)	34. (a)	35. (d)					

Practice Set 3

1. (c)	2. (c)	3. (b)	4. (c)	5. (d)	6. (c)	7. (d)	8. (a)	9. (b)	10. (c)
11. (d)	12. (a)	13. (a)	14. (d)	15. (b)	16. (c)	17. (c)	18. (a)	19. (c)	20. (c)
21. (d)	22. (d)	23. (c)	24. (a)	25. (b)	26. (b)	27. (b)	28. (a)	29. (c)	30. (d)
31. (c)	32. (a)	33. (a)	34. (a)	35. (b)					